WOOD CARVING CARICATURE PUMPKINS

By Yaron Yedidia

The Old Wood Shack LLC

Dedication
I would like to thank all the amazing caricature woodcarvers that I had the privilege to study with in the last 10 years and dedicate this book to my wife Rachel for accepting the woodchips I left all around the house.

:O) Yaron

Yaron Yedidia
Visit my website at http://www.oldwoodshack.com/

Printed in the United States of America

First Printing: April 2019

ISBN-13 978-0-578-49353-4

AUTHOR'S NOTE

I have been woodcarving for a few years now, caricatures mainly as they are forgiving. You don't really need to get the nose just the right size and if you mess up and take out an unintended extra piece of wood, you'll still have a nose just a different shape than originally intended. These figures that are made from wood are magic! You take a square piece of wood and transform it into a lovable little caricature that put a smile on everyone's face.

There are many caricature carving books out there (I should know, I probably have most of them) so it took a while before I started writing this book as I thought I would have nothing to add. Well, it turns out no one (that I know of) has written a book on how to carve caricature pumpkins, hence this book was born.

I hope you will enjoy this book at least as much as I enjoyed creating it.

Keep Carving!

Yaron

Follow my work on Facebook©: http://www.facebook.com/OldWoodShack/
And on Instagram©: http://www.instagram.com/the_old_wood_shack/

CONTENTS

PREPARING THE CUTOUT

Creating the Cutout

To make carving the caricature pumpkins a little easier, we first need to convert the basswood stick into a cutout. Working on a full stick of pumpkins (rather than cutting each one) gives us better support and keeps our hands away from the knife and tools. Preparing the cutout makes it easier to shape each pumpkin individually. In the next few steps we will turn a stick of basswood into a carveable cutout.

For the carvings you see in this book I used a $1^{1/4}$"x$1^{1/4}$" x 11" basswood. You can choose any size of square woodcarving stick that you feel comfortable holding in your hand. For the smaller quicker pumpkins use a small stick. I suggest 1" X 1" at minimum and anywhere from 1.25" to 2" at most would work best. The bigger the stick, the larger the pumpkins.

I will show two methods that can be used to mark the cutout. The first one is the one I use, yet it is less accurate. Choose whichever method that you feel works for you. Marking the wood is a crucial step that shouldn't be skipped, as the markings on the wood will guide us during the wood cutting process.

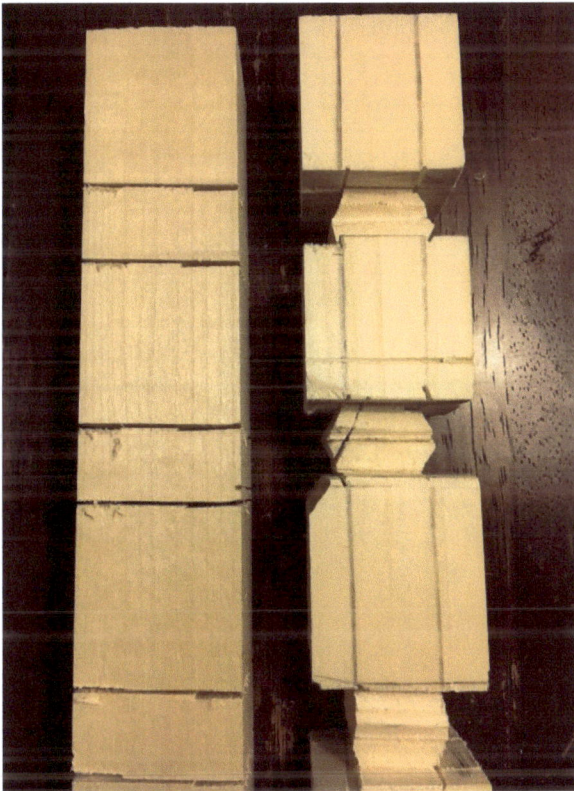

Safety First

Safety must come first. Knives, saws and other tools can cause you harm. This book does not teach you how to use the tools nor tools safety so make sure you know how to use these tools before you start.

1st Method – Quick & Dirty - Using a sketch

This method is quicker but is not as accurate. I do a quick sketch, then use the sketch to mark the wooden stick. We will begin by marking the stems of the pumpkins.

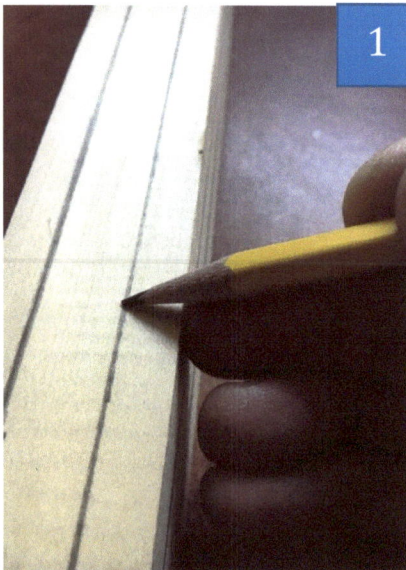

I use my figure as a guide to roughly mark 1/3 or less of the stick. Without changing the hold on the pencil, turn the wood around and mark the 2nd line as shown in photo.

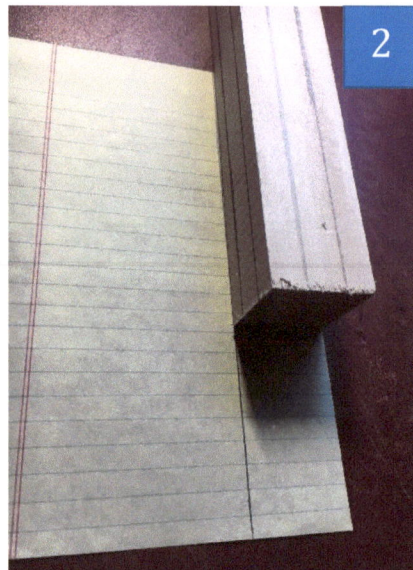

Sketch a line representing the width of the wood, this will help with sketching the pumpkin and marking the wood.

Using the width marked in the previous step, roughly sketch your pumpkin, then the stems. Mark the stem's top and bottom to lines as shown in the photo.

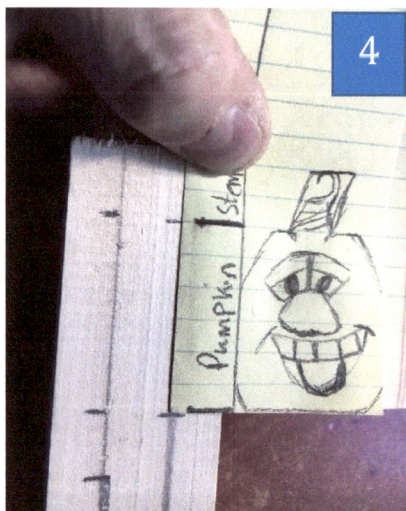

Align the sketch with the top of the wood and transfer the lines to the wood. Then use a flat piece of wood or a ruler to connect the 2 lines.

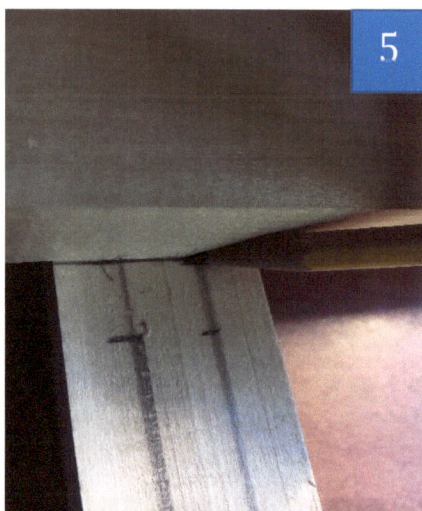

Continue to mark the lines until the last stem is in place. You might end up with a smaller pumpkin at the end or an unused area.

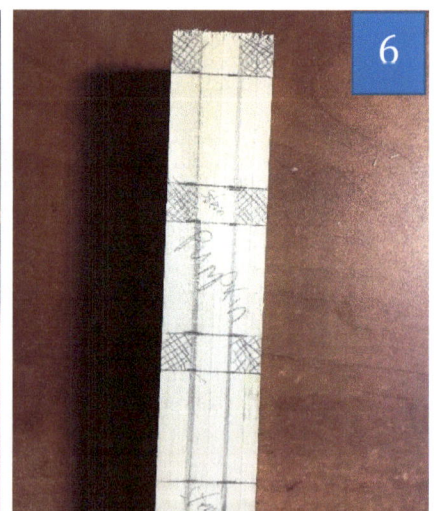

When you are done with one side, repeat the markings on at least one more side. This will help with making the cuts.

2nd method - Using a measuring tape

We will begin by marking the stems. You can make these as long or as short as you'd like. I used $1^{1/4}$"x $1^{1/4}$" with a length of 5/8" for the stem and between 1.5" to 1-3/4" for the pumpkin body. Total length is 2-1/4" so if you use a 12" long piece of wood you should get about five pumpkins with some small spare.

Measure 5/8" from the top and mark a line across the wood. Turn the wood on its side and extend the line across, repeat for all 4 sides.

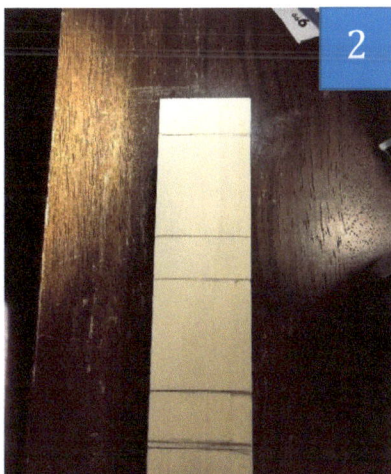

Next, measure and mark the pumpkin body. From the previous line marked, measure 1-3/4" and mark a line across. We will repeat step 1 and step 2 until the entire wood has horizontal line markings on it.

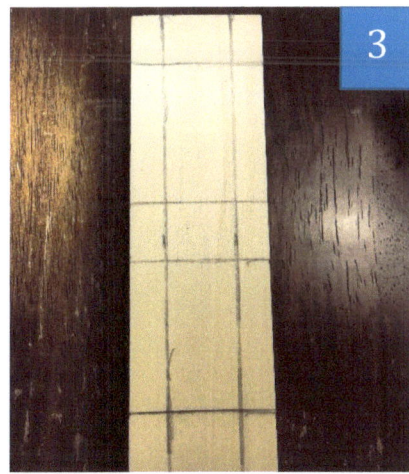

Next, measure and mark 3/8" from each side and draw a horizontal line from top to bottom across the length of the wood, repeat on all 4 sides. Once done your piece should look like this.

Cutting the wood

Once you've marked your wood we are ready to start cutting. I use a bandsaw in the example below, but a hand saw will work just as well.

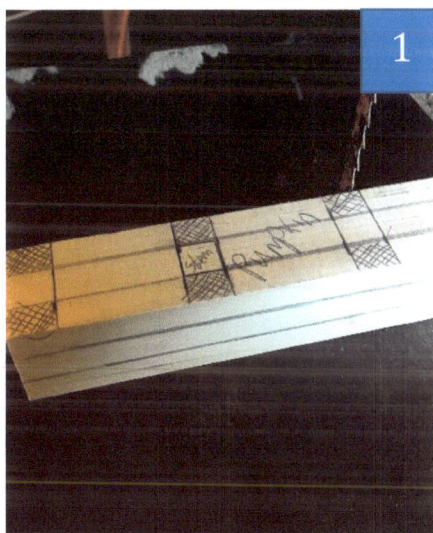

Start by removing the wood surrounding the pumpkin's stem. Use the stem's marked horizontal lines to make a cut.

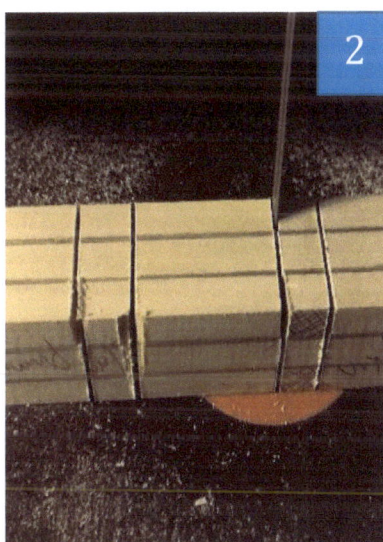

Make sure you do not go too deep. You only need to cut to the line, leaving the center intact. Go over all the lines on all four sides.

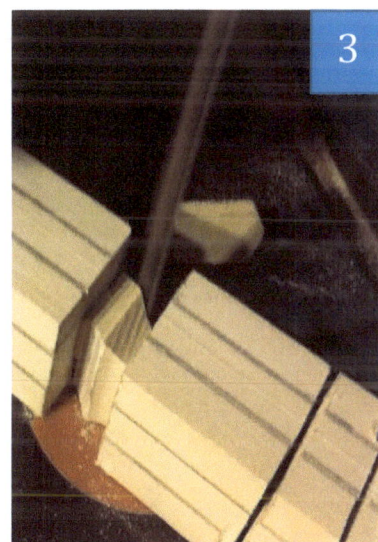

When done, either use the bandsaw or a roughout knife to remove the wood.

CARVING THE PUMPKINS

Getting ready to carve

We will use the next few steps to complete the final preparations before starting to carve.

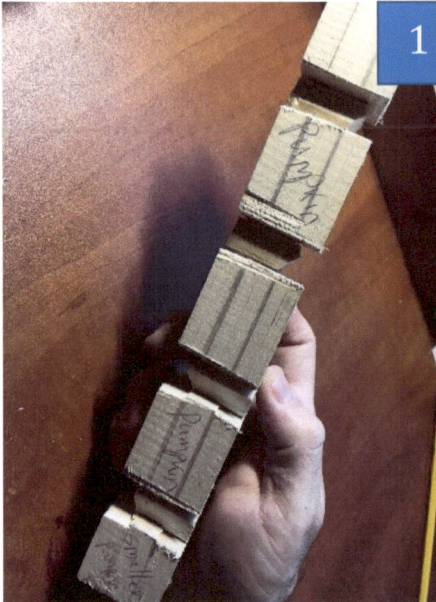

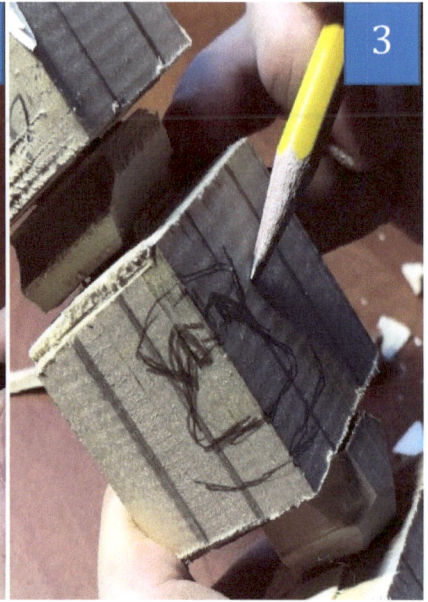

This is what your wood stick should look like now if you used the bandsaw to take out the access wood out of the stems.

We will start by taking out the corners of the wood. That will make it easier to hold. Remove the ends of the corners from all pumpkins.

If you'd like, you can sketch the outline of your pumpkin on the corner of the wood.

If you didn't use a bandsaw to remove the wood around the stem, use your roughout knife to remove it now.

Carving the Nose

Now that we have completed the preparation we are ready to start carving. We will start with the nose

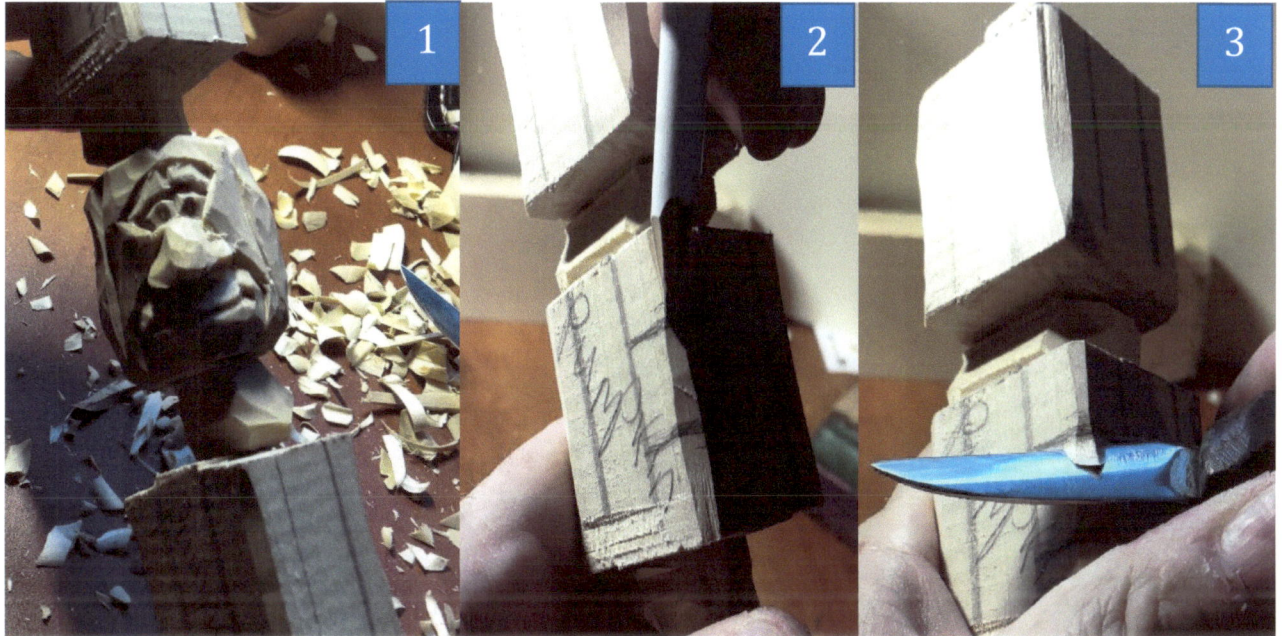

This is an example of what your pumpkin may look like once we're finished

We will start by marking the nose. Mark two lines on the corner as shown in the photo.

If you'd like, you can sketch the outline of your pumpkin on the corner of the wood.

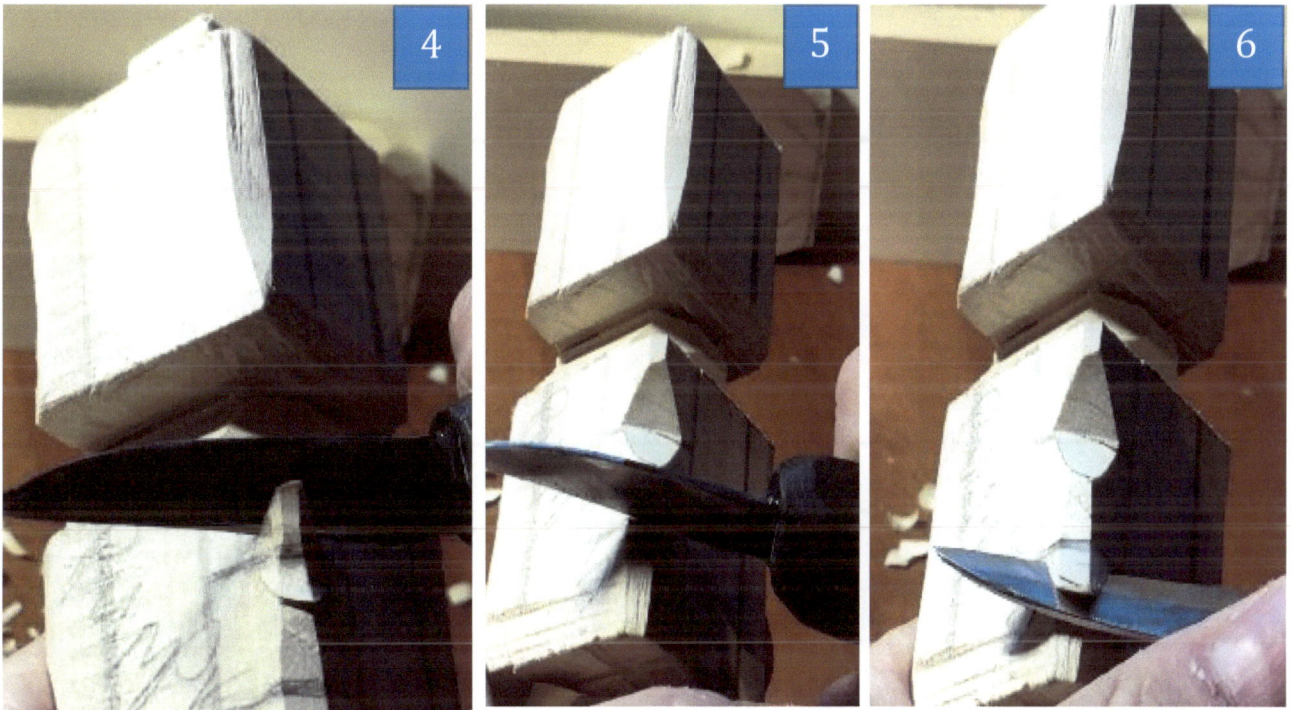

Carve to the line from the top to the line and again from the bottom to the line creating a V

Cut a stop cut at the bottom line indicating the nose bottom.

Make a cut towards the bottom of the nose to clear the wood under the nose.

This is what your carving should looks like now.

In an angle, cut some of the wood connecting between the top of the nose and the bottom.

Place your knife as shown and cut to remove the wood.

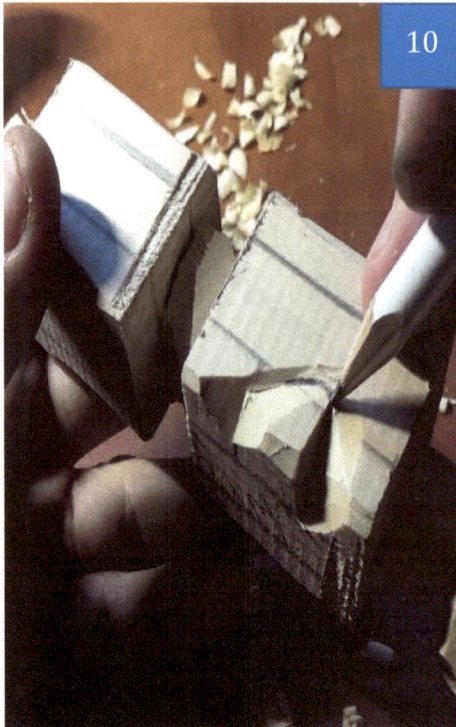

Mark the corner of the nose.

Use a knife to make a stop cut onto the traced line

Then clean out the wood by Cutting to the stop cut you just made

Take the corner of the nose.

Your pumpkin should now look like this.

Clear the wood under the nose

Clean the wood from the top of the nose to the end of the pumpkin.

Use a knife to make a stop cut onto the traced line

Carving the Eyes

Now that we have completed the nose let's continue to the eyes.

Use a pencil to mark the eyes area.

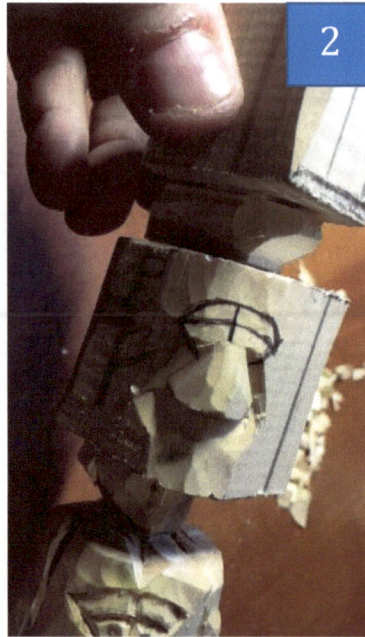

Mark the center and the bottom of the eyelids (in the center) as shown in the photo.

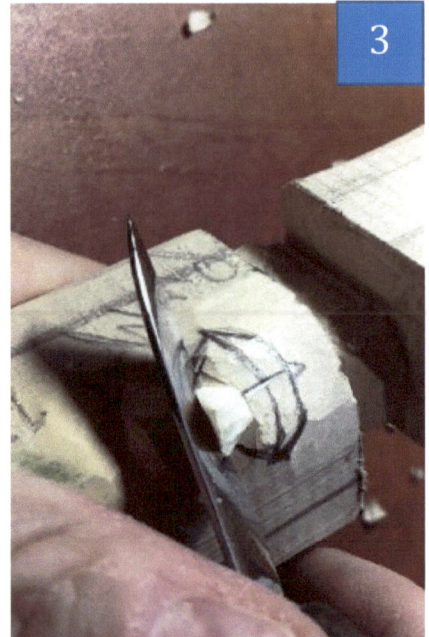

Make a cut on top of the nose towards the eye area to start a V cut.

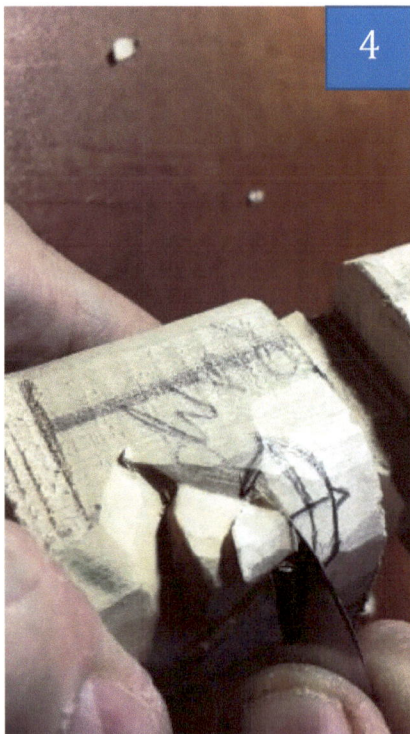

Then come back from the top to complete the V cut.

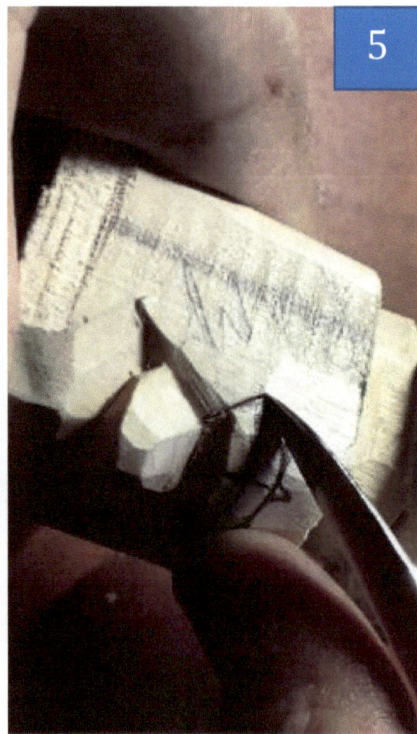

Next, start tracing the outside line with your knife, going all around the lines.

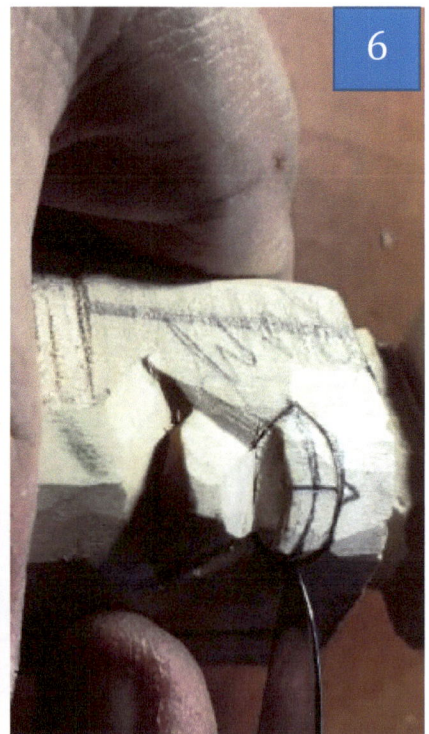

Continue to trace around the outside lines until you reach the nose.

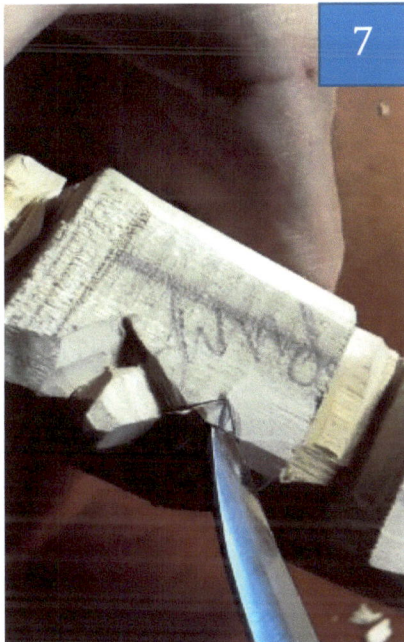

Next, cut into the corner of the eye area removing the wood working between the two cuts to complete a triangle.

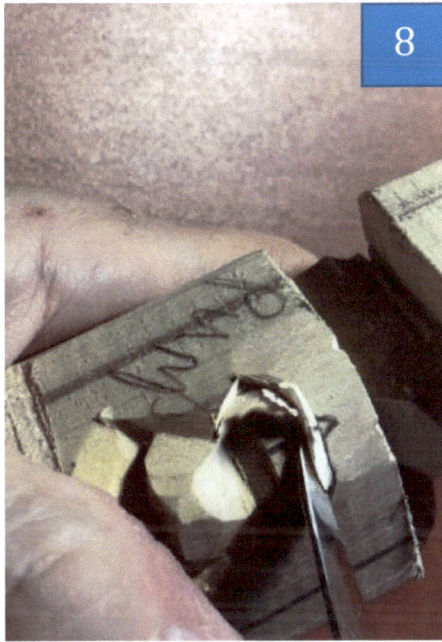

Continue to remove the wood hitting the stop cut you made earlier.

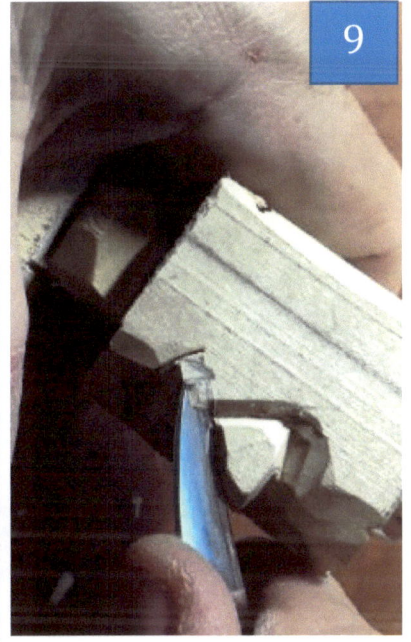

Continue to remove some wood all around the eye area

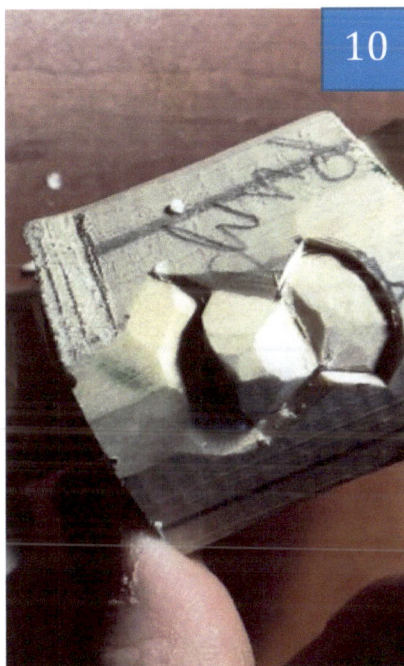

This is what your carving should look like after cleaning the eye area.

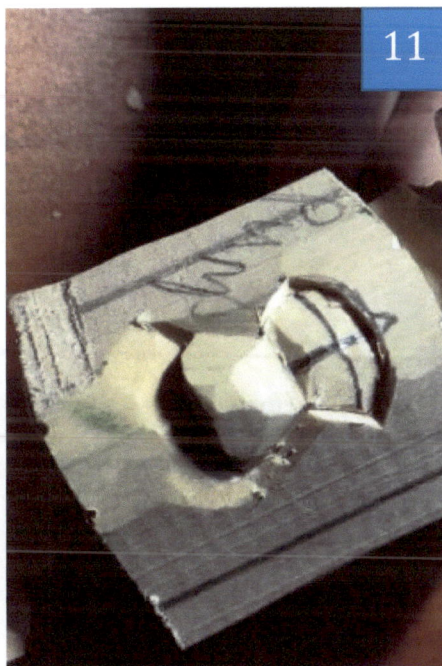

Redraw the center lines for the lids as shown in the photo.

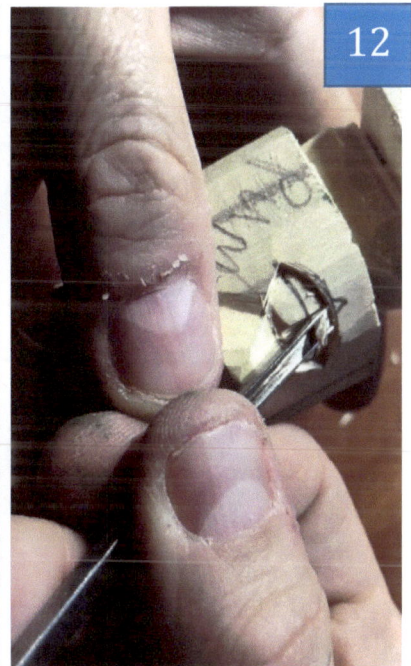

Use a small V tool to remove the wood under the line from bottom to top.

9

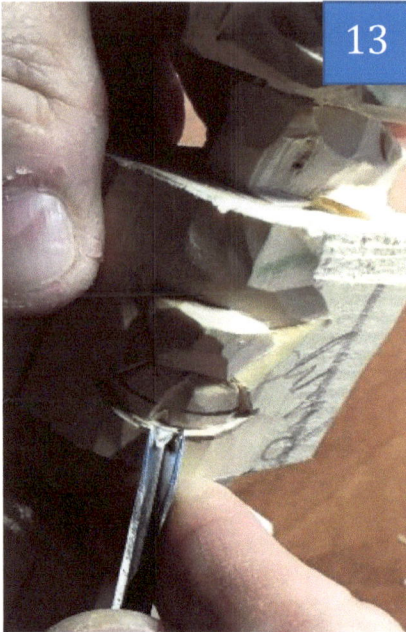

Turn the carving upside down and use the V tool to create the little V on top of the eyes area.

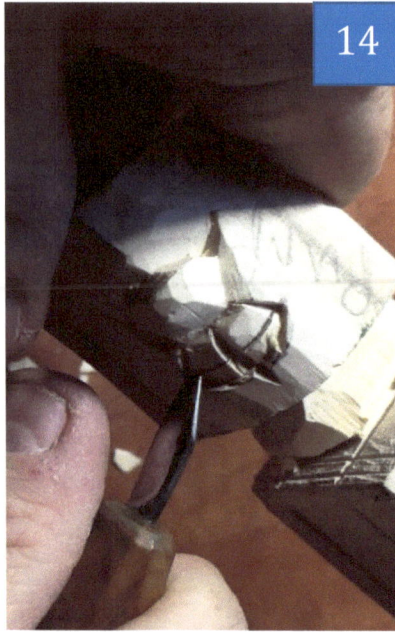

Use your knife to make a stop cut on the bottom of the lid (Half way line between the top and bottom of eye area).

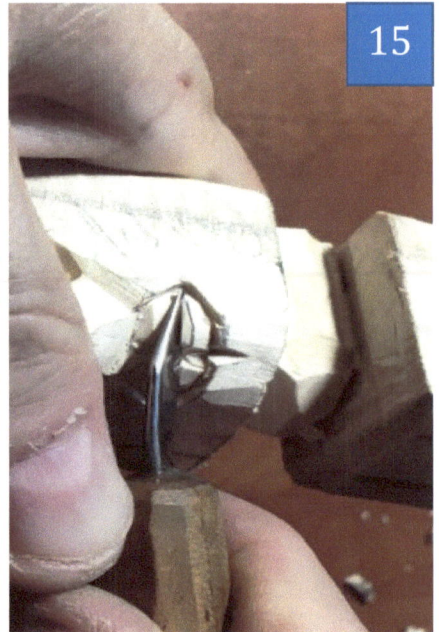

Work your way to the stop cut you just made and remove some of the wood from the top of the eye.

Continue to remove wood under the lid for the second eye

Shape the eyes to a small ball shape by removing the wood around it.

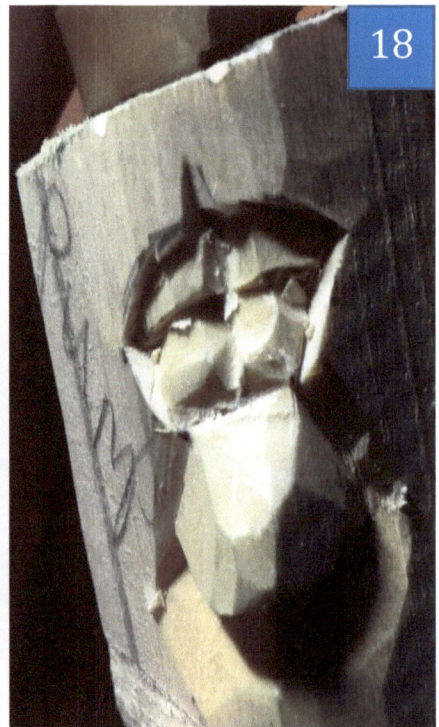

This is what your eyes should look like at this point.

Shaping the Nose and Face

Now we will work on the bottom of the nose and round the face area.

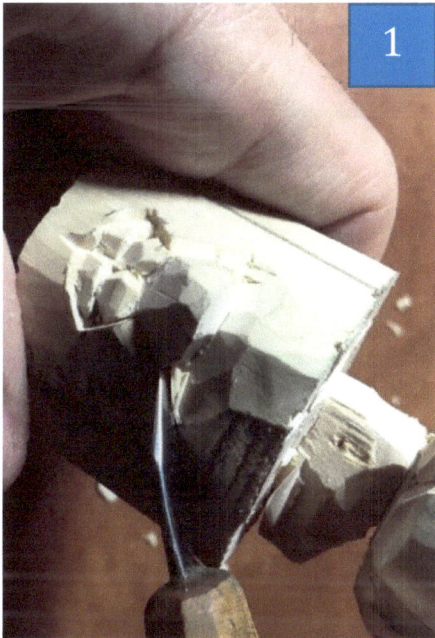

We will now make a triangle into the corner of the nose. Use your knife to make a cut from the corner of the nose towards the side bottom as shown in photo.

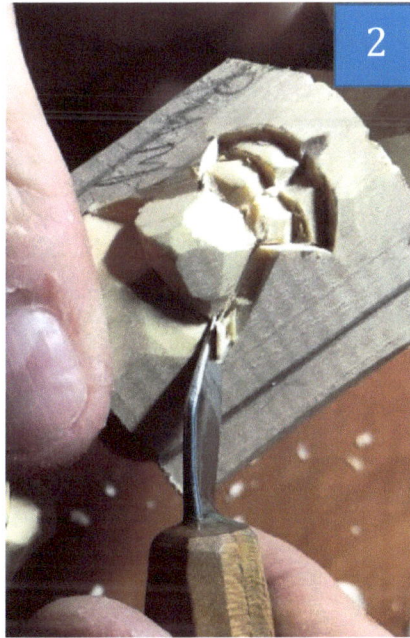

Clean the wood under the nose on the left side then continue to do the same on the right.

Next, we will make a cut into the nose to create the nostril.

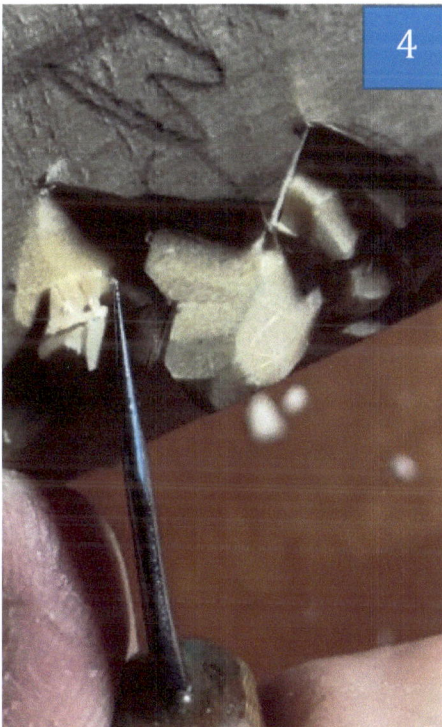

Come back from the other side creating a triangle as shown in the photo.

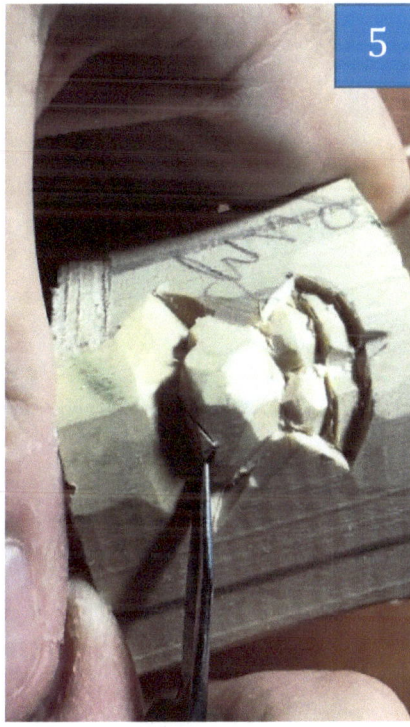

Repeat for the second nostril.

Place a gouge on the tip of the nose and push it towards the cheek (use a #5 or #3).

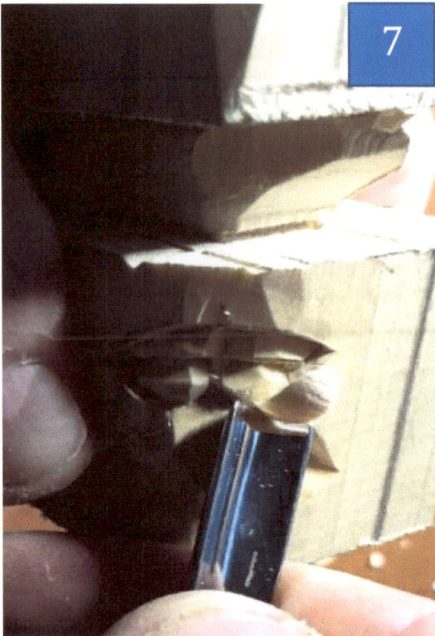

Repeat the same cut on the second side of the nose.

Now to round the outside of the nostrils, flip your gouge and run it on the side of the nose.

Repeat on the other side.

Clean up the wood that was cut by the gauge.

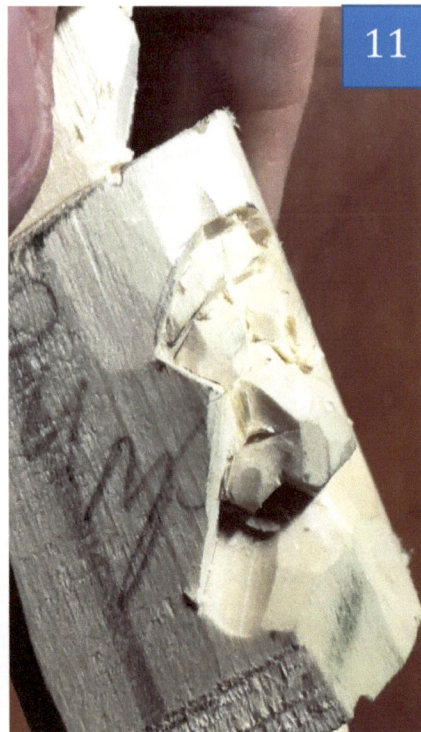

This is what your nose would look like after the last step.

Let's do some face shaping by extending the eye area and removing some wood from the face.

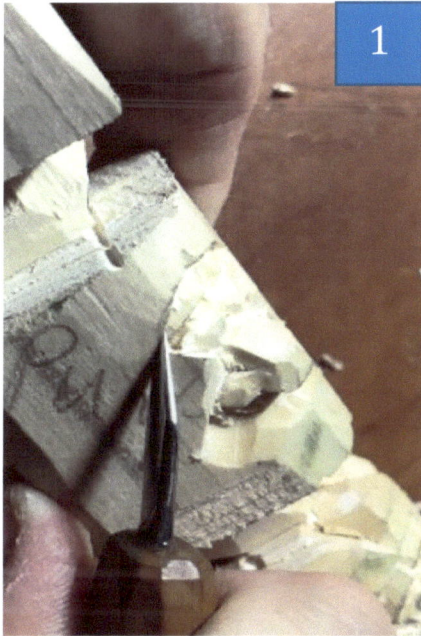

Continue the top line and extend it a bit beyond the side line

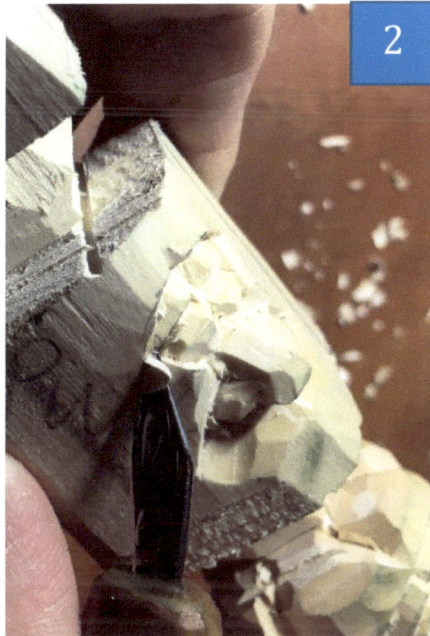

Cut into the line you just created removing the wood.

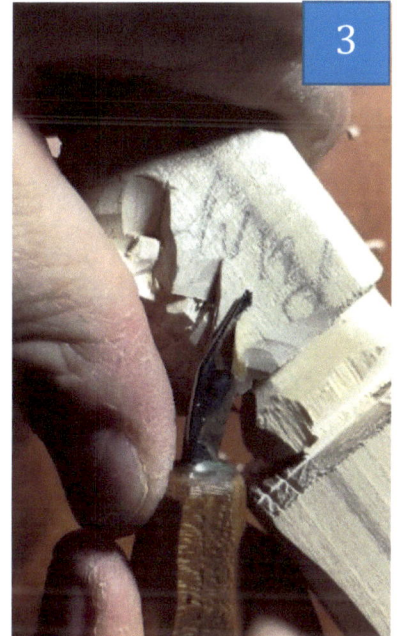

Clear some wood above the eye.

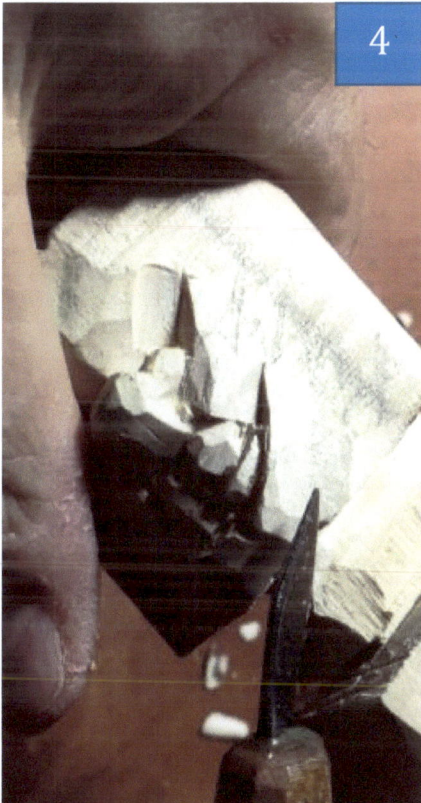

This is what your eye would look like after the last step.

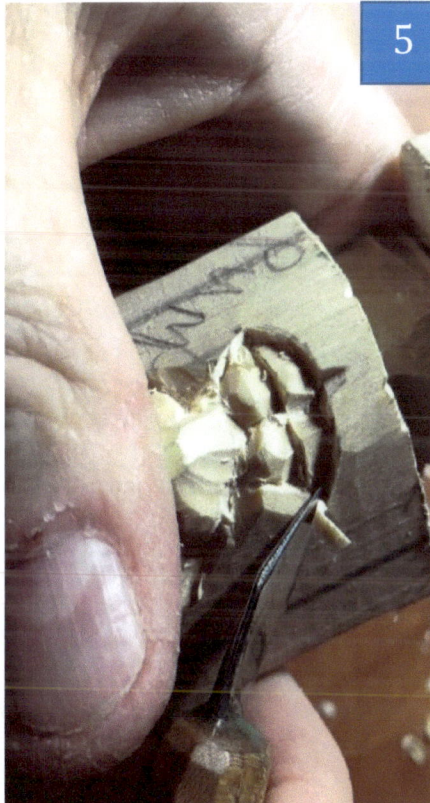

Repeat on the other side. Take out some wood from the corner of the other eye.

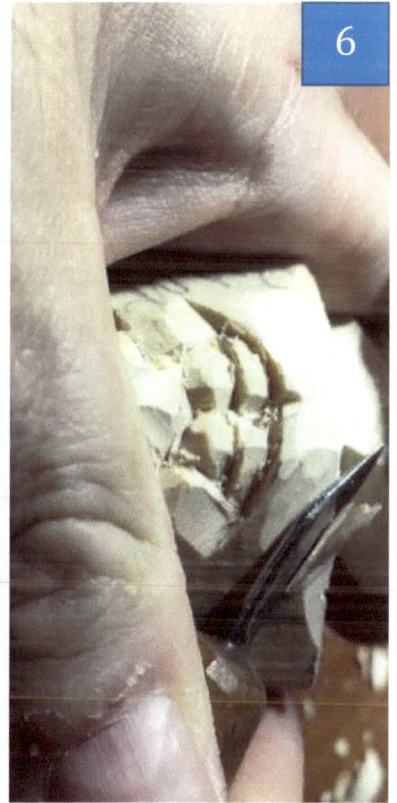

Remove some wood above the right eye to round the area.

Carving the mouth

Let's start carving out the mouth

Start by marking the pumpkin's mouth.

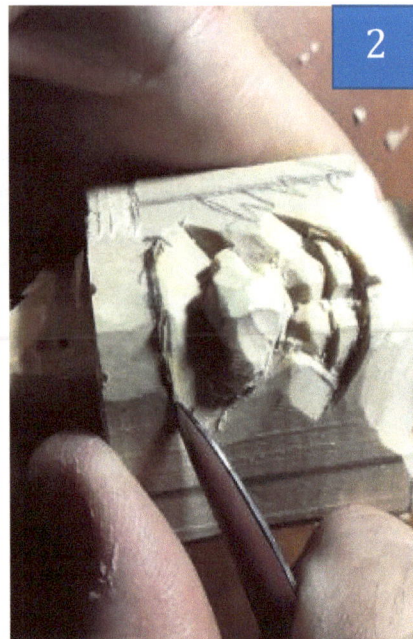

Run your knife from above towards the marked line to make a stop cut.

Now cut up to the line you just created from the bottom.

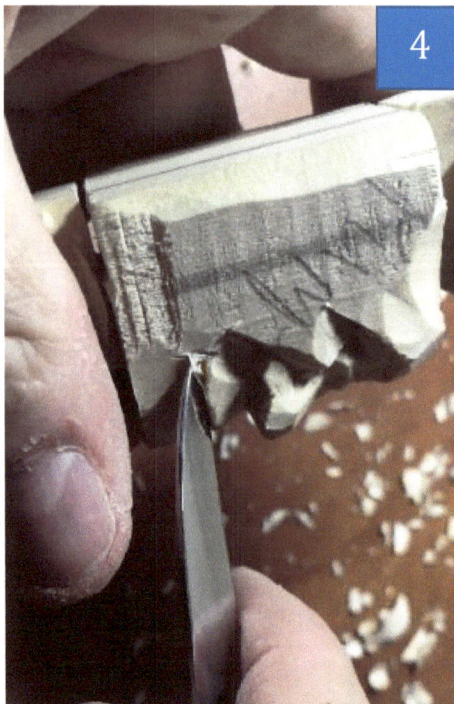

At the corner of the mouth we will cutout a triangle. This will require three cuts. Make the first cut on the bottom of the triangle

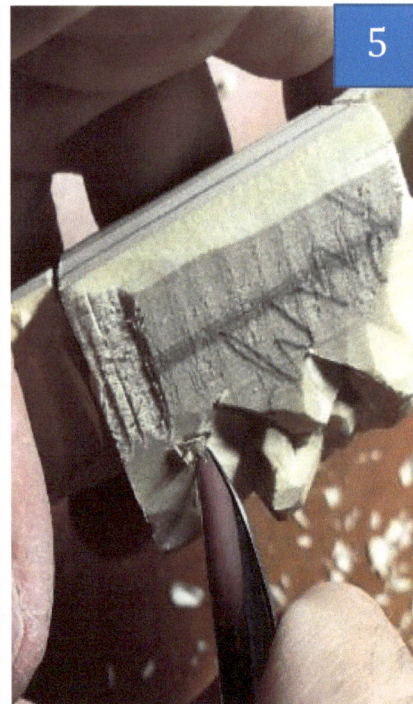

Make the second cut from the top.

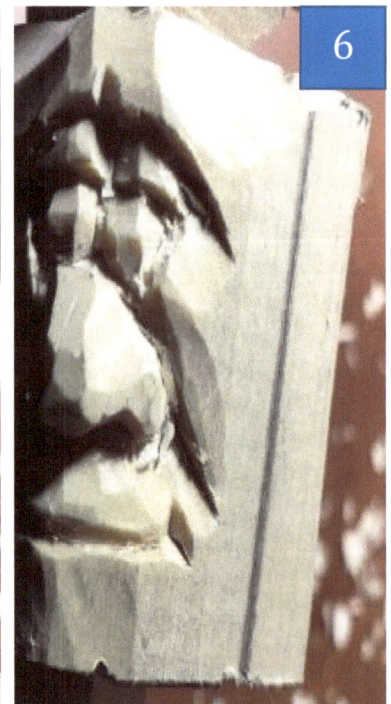

The third cut will release the little triangle. You can practice cutting a triangle on a separate piece of wood. Repeat on other side.

Your carved mouth would look like this now.

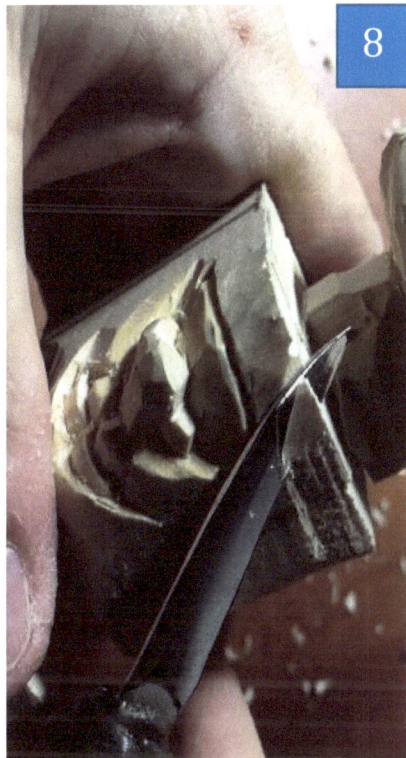
Clean some wood from the bottom of the pumpkin as shown.

Repeat on the other side to form the chin.

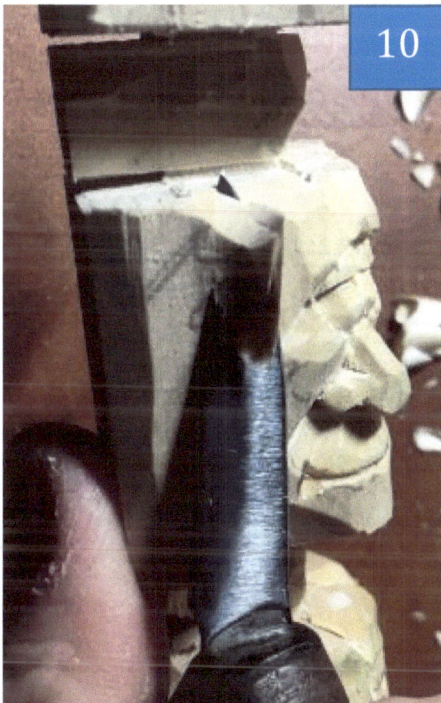
Let's start cleaning and forming the pumpkin shape. Take some wood out from the top right and left of the pumpkin.

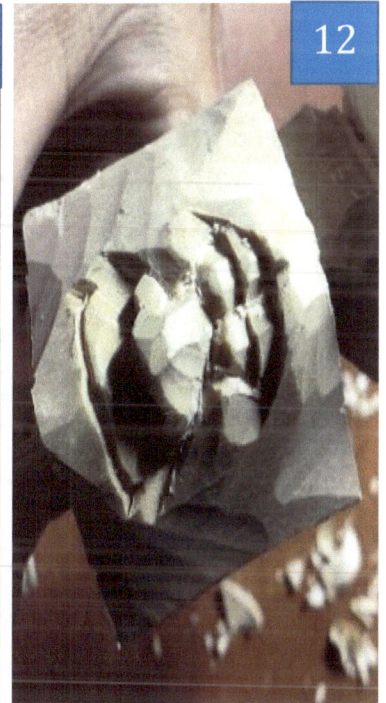
At this stage your pumpkin will look like this.

Shaping the pumpkin

Next let's work on shaping the pumpkin

Remove some wood from the side of the pumpkin to form the pumpkin shape.

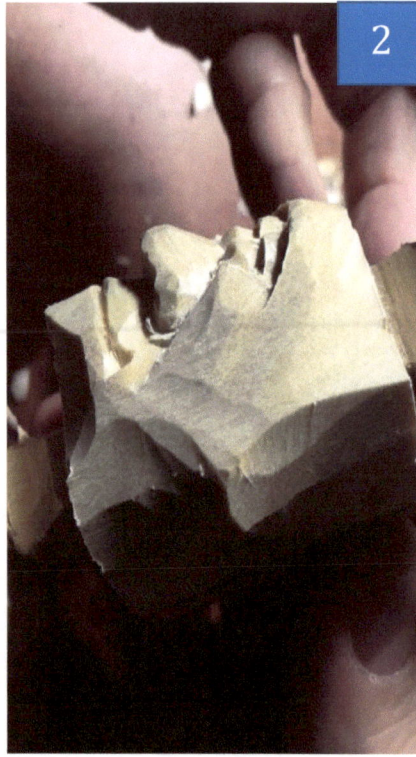

Work from the center to the top then flip the pumpkin and take some wood from the center to the bottom.

Repeat on the other side.

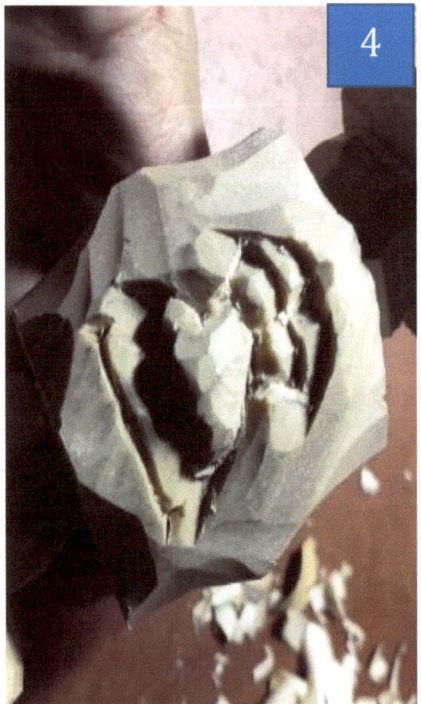

Start making a V cut by cutting into the line you created from one side.

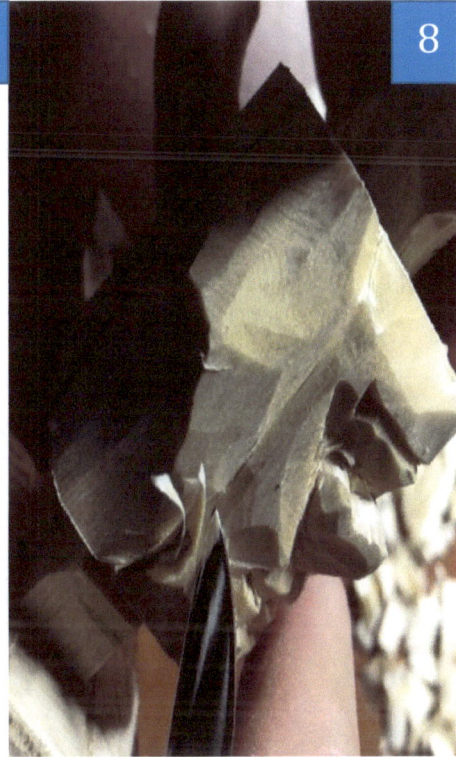

Then come back from the other side to complete the V cut.

Repeat on all sides then cut a small triangle at the end of each line.

Repeat the cleaning process on the back side.

Your pumpkin should look like this.

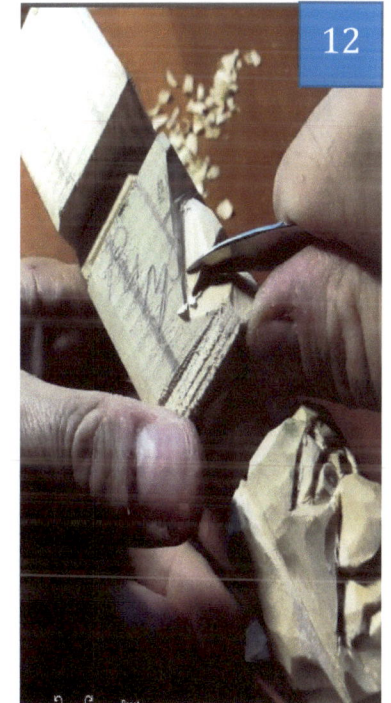

Now you are ready to Continue and carve all the rest of your pumpkins on the stick.

Next we will complete the final shaping of the pumpkin and stems.

Separate the pumpkins by using a roughout knife or a saw.

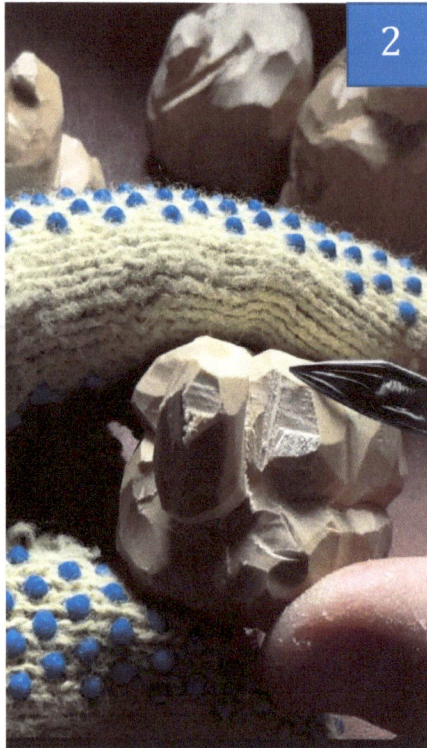

Clean the top by removing the bandsaw cutting marks.

Repeat on all the top bumps and the stem.

Your final pumpkin is ready for paint

PAINTING & FINISHING

Preparing to paint

A good method for painting your wood carvings is using acrylic paint that is thinned down with water. I use a few drops of acrylic paint mixed with water. The more water you use the less paint will end up on your carving. You can start with testing your paint on a separate piece of wood. If your paint comes out too thin you can always add another drop of paint into the mix.

I start by extracting 2-3 drops of paint with the color of choice then adding a few drops of water and mixing, then adding more drops of water while continuing to mix. These paint pallets are relatively inexpensive and can be purchased in any hobby store. The water container can be purchased in the supermarket aisle in the travel section where they sell small bottle shaving cream and shampoos for travelers.

When applying the diluted acrylic paint you might notice the results are dull and the color isn't really standing out – do not worry this is normal and once you get to the end and apply the Boiled Linseed Oil these colors will pop and make your woodcarving shine.

The technique I use is just one way to paint and finish your carvings. You can use whatever works for you, I know some woodcarvers use clear coat finish prior to painting that reduces the paint sipping into other sections.

Use whichever brand of acrylic paint you can get. For the simple pumpkins we will need, Orange, white, Green and red.	After shaking the paint container to mix the paint, squeeze out a couple of paint drop and then thin them down with water	You can try it on a scrap piece of wood before applying to your final carving. Because I want the green to be stronger I use not as much water as I use for the orange.

Apply the diluted paint onto the surfaces of the pumpkin, try to avoid the eyes, stem and teeth as these will have be painted different colors.

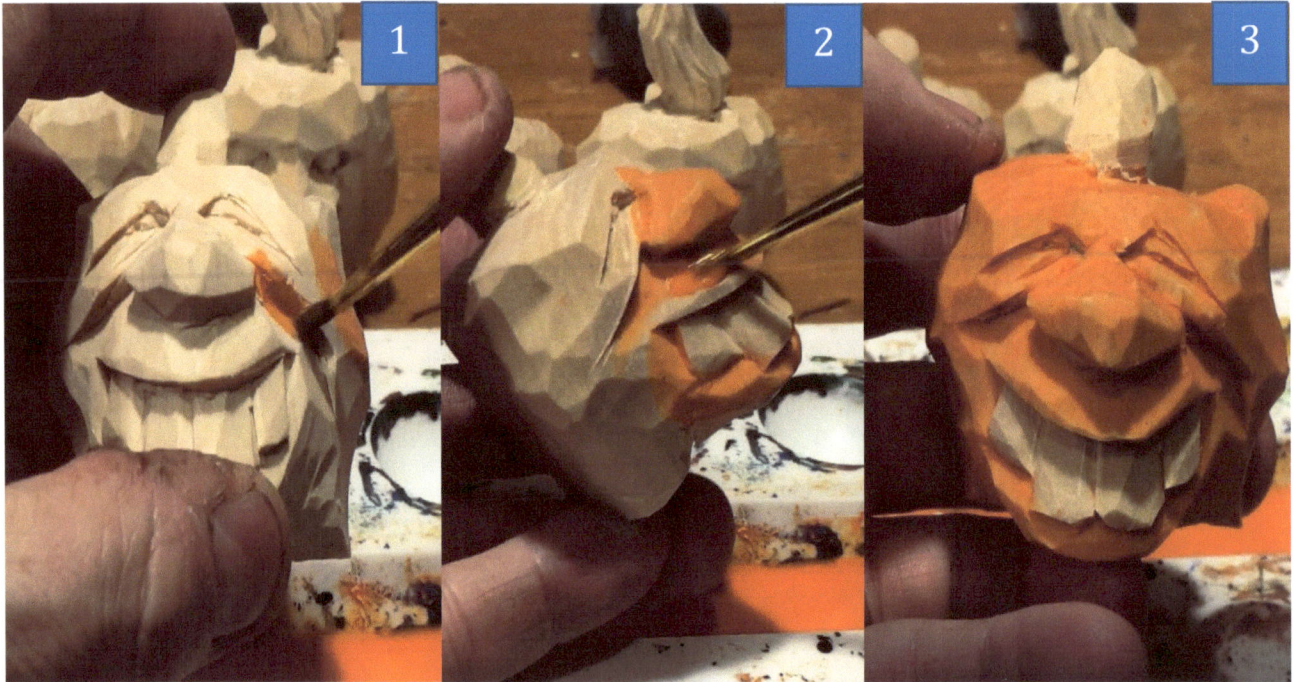

Use a nice size brush to apply the paint, since the paint is thinned down with water the grain will show.

Work your way around the entire face.

Continue to apply to the rest of the pumpkin.

The orange color should go on all the pumpkins you just carved.

Coloring the eyes and teeth

Now let's paint the eyes. We use the white paint without diluting. Use the right size of brush depending on eye size.

Make sure your brush is fully covered with white paint, then remove some of the paint.

With small slow strokes fill in the eye area.

Continue to apply the white paint on the other eye

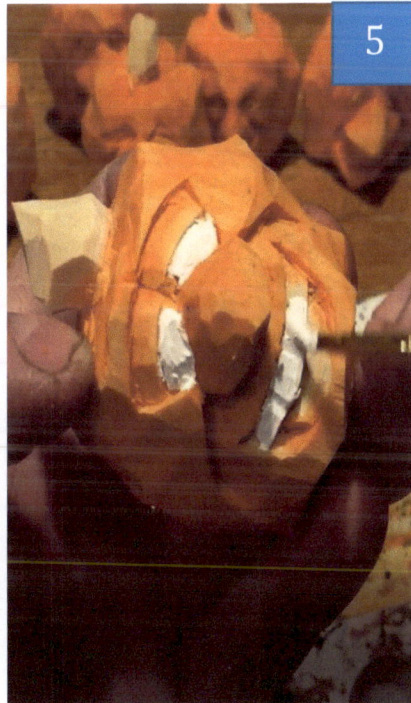

Then proceed to paint the teeth. If you want you can use a drop of water and dip your brush into the drop for just a bit of diluting.

Your pumpkin should look like this. Continue to paint all your other pumpkins with the white color.

Coloring the stem & Mouth area

Mix the green color paint with some water.

Apply the green paint onto the stem. Some paint may seep into the top of the pumpkin but that is ok.

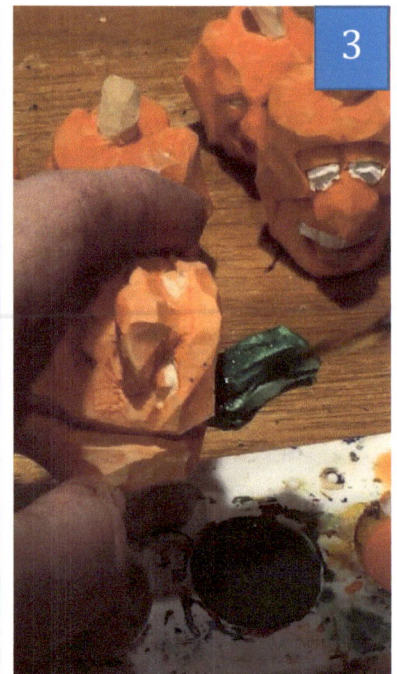

Work your way around the entire stem. If it is too light either add some paint into the water or wait for it to dry then apply a second coat.

If you need to go back and fix or cover an area, use some less diluted paint as needed.

Use a diluted red on the tongue area

Your pumpkin should look like this. Continue to paint all your other pumpkins with the white color.

Coloring the Eyes

1

We will use the black color acrylic paint out of the box without diluting. Apply color to your brush and remove excess paint.

2

I paint the eyes at either corner of the pumpkin, which makes them appear as if they were looking to the side or up.

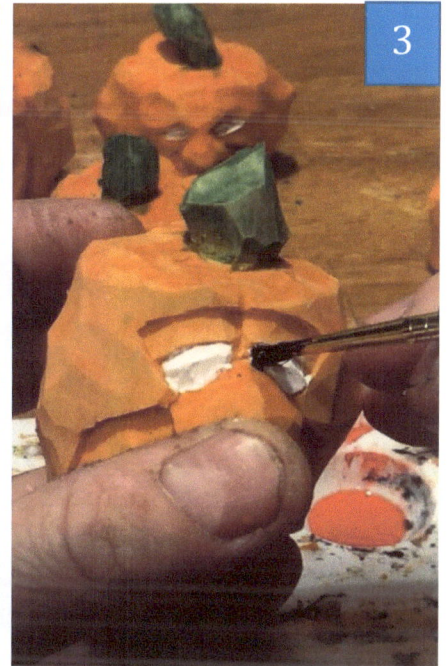

3

Press your brush onto the corner and roll it around carefully. Notice how I stabilize my brush by pressing the little finger onto the pumpkin for extra support.

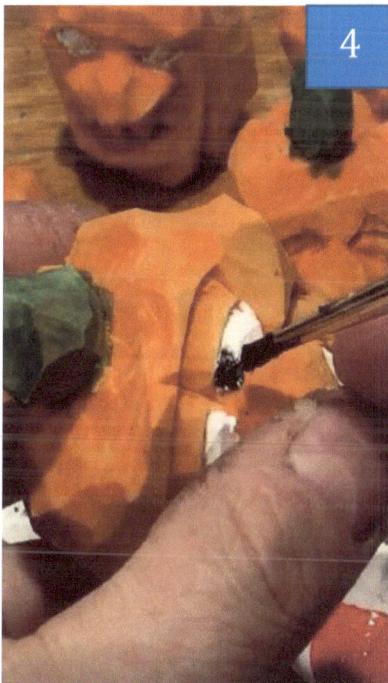

4

Create a little circle in the left corner of the right eye

5

Then repeat on the left corner of the left eye. Try to match the size to the right eye.

6

Continue to the rest of the pumpkins, you can alternate the location of the pupil both left both right or even one left and one right. Let the paint dry.

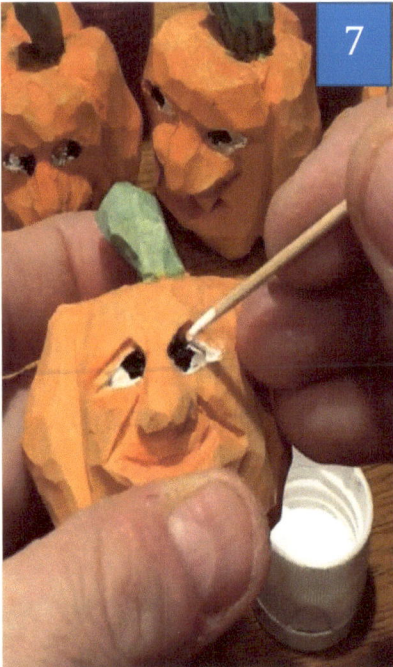

For the last step we will place a small white dot on the pupil. Use a toothpick, dip it into the white color paint.

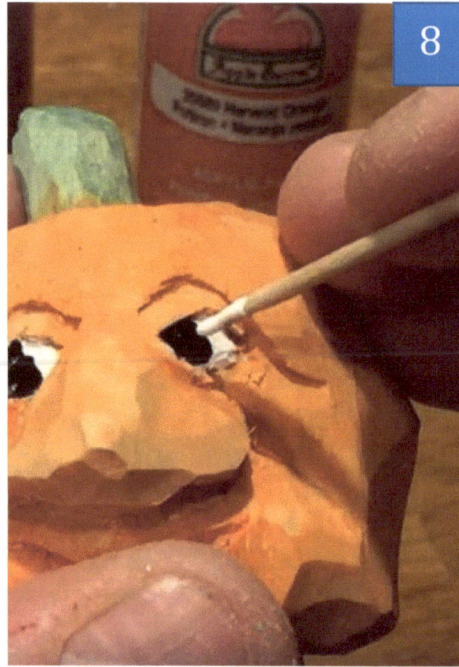

Place the dot on the right top side of the pupil

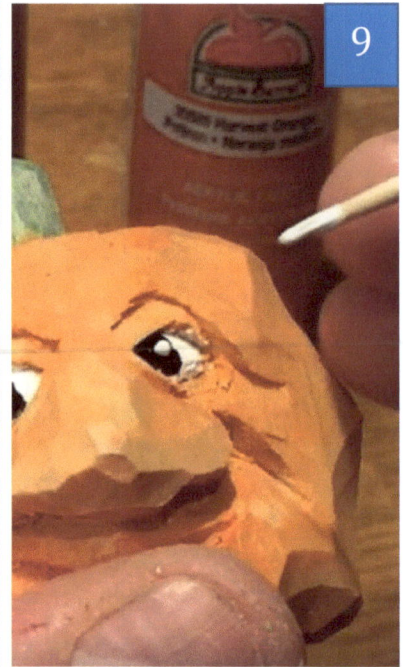

You'll need enough paint to simply place that tiny dot inside the pupil. Stabilize your touch by placing your little finger and pushing against the carving. Repeat on the second eye. Then on all your pumpkins.

If you smeared the white dot, don't worry, wait until it dries then go back with a black paint on a tooth pick and clean it up.

This is what your pumpkins should look like at this stage. Remember the colors look dull but don't worry once we get them through the boiled linseed oil they will shine and the colors will pop!

Boiled Linseed Oil

Boiled linseed oil is a great oil to finish your woodcarvings with. It takes the dull colors and make them pop. It does have some odor that disappears after a few days. Also, make sure you read the warning label before using, it is suggested to use gloves when handling boiled linseed oil and specially to dispose the left-over absorbent paper or rugs in a bag with some water as these rags have been known to combust and cause fires. Place them in a bag and pour some water on them close the bag before disposing.

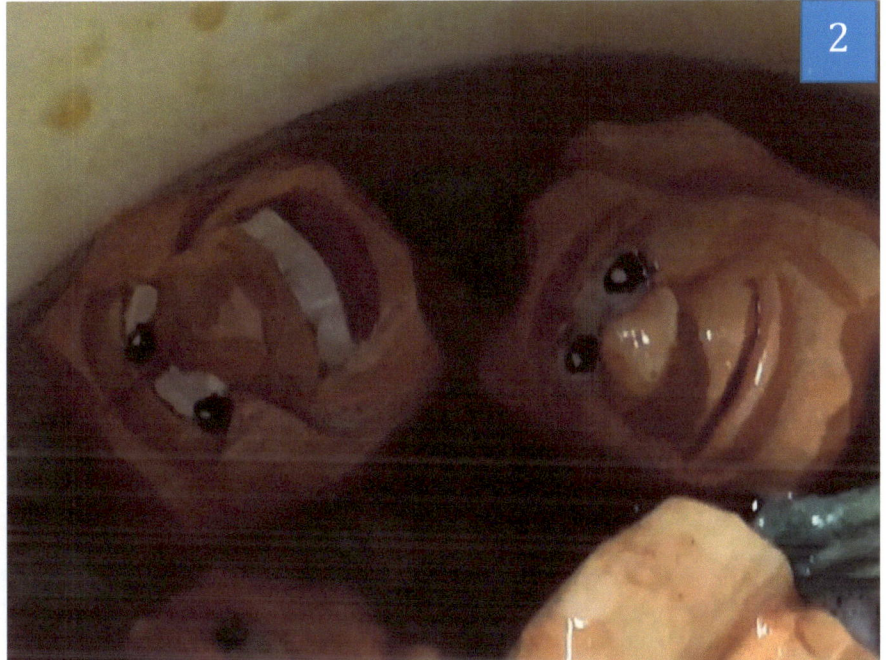

I use Boiled Linseed Oil to finish the pumpkins. You can either use the oil out of the box or mix it with some burnt amber (some Oil paint with paint thinner then mix with oil)

Use a bucket to soak the pumpkins in or simply brush the oil on them. Take them out of the bucket let the excess oil drip back into the bucket then place them on absorbent paper.

Leave them for at least 15 minutes before wiping off the excess oil.

This is what your pumpkins should look like at this stage (before wiping them down).

EXAMPLES

Checkout the great work of other woodcarvers

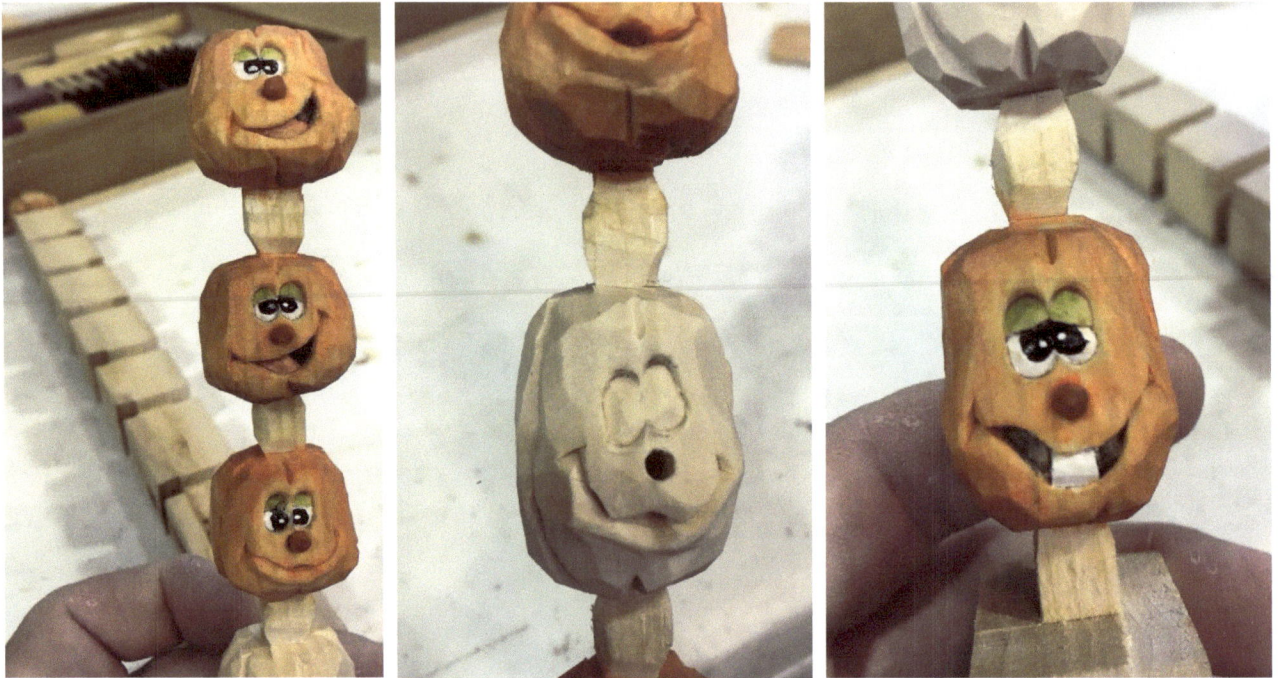

Rod Beamish from Bremen, IN showed me how to start carving pumpkins on a stick. He has a special technique where he drills a hole for the nose and fills it with a small dowel. He also carves the eyes as the figure 8 sideways then uses green for the eye lids and carves the stem separately then attach it back on. Here are some of his great wood carved pumpkins.

Here are some tips from Rob: The little stick is the stems. After I separated a pumpkin I would carve the top and then recess where the stem would be with a gouge, frill a 1/8 or 3/16 hole and then carve the stick to fit. I carve a rough shape for the stem as shown on the stick, glue and put in the hole then break it off and finish carving and shaping a stem. Sure easier and better end result. I carved a nose and shallow eye channel. The larger stick was left square on one corner for that purpose and as you can see the corners were knocked off. If I didn't carve a nose I used those 1/4 inch wood buttons or 1/4 inch plugs. You can get them at a wood shop/hobby stores.

Bruce Ankeny from Blue Earth MN carved these wonderful pumpkins they are called "Punks"

Bigger Size Pumpkins

You might want to carve bigger pumpkins, here are some options

Choose the size you want to carve. The best size would be the one you can fit in your hand so you can still use the hand tools you use for the smaller woodcarvings.

Use the same steps we learned earlier on the smaller pumpkins and be creative with the different eye / nose / mouth combinations.

www.ingramcontent.com/pod-product-compliance
Lightning Source LLC
LaVergne TN
LVHW072122070426
835511LV00002B/60